Lead That Thing!

COPYRIGHT © 2020 By Aruna Krishnan

All Rights Reserved. This book or any portion thereof may not be reproduced or used in any manner whatsoever without the express written permission of the publisher except for the use of brief quotations in a book review.

Lead That Thing!

Leadership for a Busy Mind

By Aruna Krishnan

DEDICATION

This book is dedicated to my mother-in-law who was a true leader in so many ways.

You had a positive impact on so many lives.

You were always ready to help anyone in need.

You will be missed dearly.

ACKNOWLEDGEMENTS

It's hard to believe this is my third book! I have had a lot of encouragement and support from a number of people. This fuels my passion for writing books that help others with personal development. I would like to thank the people who have been a part of this journey.

My husband, for his support and confidence in me.

My kids, for giving me my first leadership role... Motherhood. It has taught me a lot!

Family and friends, who gave me feedback on my previous book. You have helped me further my craft as an author.

My friends in the Polka Dot Powerhouse and eWomenNetwork, for taking an interest in my journey as an author.

The leaders who provided insights into their leadership journeys - Rick Parks, Bill Bunzel, Holly Lifke, Andy Weins, Brenda Campbell, and Rashi Khosla.

My editor, cover designer and book formatter for bringing this book to life.

Thank you!

"If your actions inspire others to dream more, learn more, do more, and become more, you are a leader."

-John Quincy Adams

TABLE OF CONTENTS

Acknowledgements v

Preface ix

Section 1: Lead That Thing! - The Wild 1

    Chapter 1: Leading Like Wolves 3

    Chapter 2: Leading Like Cheetahs 7

    Chapter 3: Leading Like Giraffes 11

Section 2: Lead That Thing! - Start With You 17

    Chapter 4: Assess Your Comfort Level 19

    Chapter 5: At Work 25

    Chapter 6: In The Community 29

    Chapter 7: At Home 33

    Chapter 8: At School 39

Section 3: Lead That Thing! With Integrity And Grit 45

    Chapter 9: Leadership... What It Is Not! 47

Chapter 10: Leaders Vs. Managers 53

Chapter 11: Influence Vs. Authority 59

Section 4: Lead That Thing! The Real World 63

Chapter 12: Rick Parks 65

Chapter 13: D. Holly Lifke 67

Chapter 14: Andy Weins 71

Chapter 15: Rashi Khosla 77

Chapter 16: Brenda Campbell 81

Chapter 17: Bill Bunzel 85

Epilogue 89

About the Author 91

PREFACE

"If you were an animal, what would you be?" This is the interview question that inspired me to write this book.

The point of this question is to understand how you see yourself as a leader and how you would function as part of a team. In one of my Toastmaster speeches, I addressed this question with an animal called WOCHEEGI; a wolf, cheetah, and giraffe. Each of these animals has a different style of leadership that has evolved over time. Aggregating their strengths gives us a solid list of leadership principles that can easily be adopted by organizational leaders too!

The book explores leadership, what it is, what it is not, and how we can learn from leaders both in the wild and in the human world. Whether you are a student, parent, professional or community leader, there is a growing need for good leadership. This book provides insights into how to further your leadership journey.

SECTION 1

Lead That Thing! - The Wild

Have you ever wondered how animals survive in the wild? Instinct plays a big part in their success, but they also have leadership skills we can draw from.

This section looks at the leadership behaviors of wolves, cheetahs, and giraffes. It draws a parallel between the leadership skills present in the natural world and how we can apply the same behavioral aspects in organizations.

CHAPTER 1

LEADING LIKE WOLVES

Wolves have a very majestic appearance. They appear self-assured, confident, and give out the "Don't mess with me" vibe. As predators, it is important for wolves to show these traits because these strengths are what make them successful as a pack.

Think about the wolf pack as a team:

- The team leader can be equated to the alpha-male of a wolf pack.
- The team members are akin to the rest of the pack.

There is a mutual dependency between the pack and the alpha male. The success of the pack depends on three things:

LEAD THAT THING!

1. The ability of the alpha to set the direction or goal - The confidence and presence of a strong leader to recognize an opportunity and lead its pack in the pursuit.
2. The skills and synergy of the pack - Each wolf in the pack has to bring its best when it comes to a hunt.
3. Trust between the pack and the alpha - Without this element, there is little to no chance of success.

Setting the Direction

From a leadership aspect, the alpha wolf selects the prey to target but does not pursue it alone. Perhaps if the prey were small, doing so alone would be considered, but in most cases, wolves prefer to pursue larger prey which requires the participation of the whole pack.

The alpha identifies the opportunity and engages his pack to go along. The strategy is usually consistent - seek out the youngest, weakest, oldest, or most accessible target as a way to ensure that effort is only expended on an attainable quest.

This is comparable to leaders in an organization determining a vision and strategy or seeking market opportunities that could result in revenue growth for the company. However, they cannot attain success without the support of a team of talented people.

Skills and Synergy

The individuals within the pack have specific roles to play during the hunt. Some are much more in the thick of the action, while others may be in more of a supportive role and stay on the sidelines. However, each role is important in building and maintaining the health and skill level of the pack.

The same applies to organizations. Each player has a critical part to play in the success of the company, regardless of where they stand in the "chain of command". It is the responsibility of the leaders in the company to ensure that each person understands this to promote employee satisfaction and retention.

Mutual Trust and Respect

There is a clear hierarchy within wolf packs with an alpha at the top of the totem pole, and an omega at the bottom. Within the team hierarchy there is still acknowledgement of each wolf's role and worth. Every wolf plays an important role in its "society".

It is important for leaders in the workplace to respect the individuals and teams that help them achieve corporate goals. Taking them for granted and abusing them with bad working conditions reduces trust and loyalty.

A weakness in the Wolf Leadership strategy

So far, I have highlighted a few things that make wolves good leaders. There is an important point to note though. The average success rate of a wolf hunt is said to be anywhere from three to fifteen percent. That is very low! With all the good things they have going for them, you would expect more success, right?

It appears that, per some studies, this failure can be attributed to their lack of coordination and communication. That's rather shocking, isn't it?

We see this issue in organizations as well. Communication across the organization is critical. The lack of transparency at any level only results in projects going awry with unnecessary repetition of work or scrapped projects. Communication is something we need to pay particular attention to so we can function more efficiently and increase our chances of success.

To summarize, take a look at the table below which compares the leadership traits required by both an organizational leader and an alpha wolf.

Organizational Leader vs. Alpha Wolf

Trait	Organizational Leader	Alpha Wolf
Direction	Sets vision and goals and creates teams to make those a reality	Determines the target and leads the pack on the hunt
Synergy	Depends on the teams and their leaders to work towards the goals	Leverages the strengths of the pack to maximize the probability of success
Mutual Trust and Respect	Needs to empower and trust the teams on the ground so their talent is best utilized	Allows the rest of the pack to use their skills and conquer as a group

In the next chapter, we take a look at a predator that has a higher hunt success rate… the cheetah.

CHAPTER 2

LEADING LIKE CHEETAHS

When my son was in kindergarten, he brought back a piece of art that was a drawing of a cheetah. The caption under that picture was "The cheetah is my favorite animal because it can run very fast." Ah, the innocence of a five-year-old!

We all know that the cheetah is the fastest animal on land. This is one of its very obvious advantages. But this strength alone is not what makes a cheetah successful. The cheetah has to be very strategic about the use of this skill. It has to consider:

- What situations require speed - Speed is not the solution to all problems.
- When and how to use speed - Speed may only be a part of a solution. It commonly needs to be

combined with heightened senses, stealth, and use of camouflage.
- The limitations of its speed - A cheetah cannot maintain maximum speed indefinitely. The acceleration element should be optimally planned out.

For animals, like the cheetah, most of these decisions are instinctual by virtue of being a part of the wild. However, as humans, we require a little more contemplation on the best use of our strengths.

Knowing when, where and how to use your strengths

There are a few stages to a cheetah hunt - detect, stalk, approach, chase, and capture. Of all these stages the only one that requires speed is the "chase". Therefore, speed is best preserved for that part of the hunt. This is the cheetah's way of strategizing.

Leaders in an organization must also strategize on the decisions they make regarding the organization. What may be a no-brainer decision at one time of the year may bring disastrous results at any other time. For example, retailers need to make special accommodations for seasonal peaks during Thanksgiving or Christmas. The plans for ramping up in terms of people, process and technology are typically only sustainable for a short period. Maintaining this standard throughout the year would hurt the company and employee morale.

While retail leaders have the opportunity to strategize on how to make seamless transitions between seasonal peaks and the rest of the year, other leaders have similar opportunities to strategize on processes specific to their industry or organization. Real leaders shine in terms of coming up with new ideas on how to be more efficient.

Knowing the limitations of your strength

The cheetah knows it can only run at high speeds for short bursts of time. This is why it gets close to its prey before giving chase and then pouncing on it. It recognizes the importance of conserving its power for effectiveness.

Similarly, we can think about an organization's product distribution strategies. A single channel, such as a traditional brick and mortar store, would limit their revenue stream and put a burden on that channel. The reliance on the single channel results in inefficiencies and ultimately, a loss of customers. Organizations need to accommodate multiple channels such as mobile and e-commerce i.e. online sales to effectively grow their customer base and sales.

Learning from the cheetah's success rate

The cheetah's hunt success rate is said to be around fifty percent. That is pretty impressive when compared to the wolf's rate of success. This is attributable to the cheetah's skills and strategic approach. Since the cheetah is generally a lone hunter, it does not need to deal with the coordination and communication aspects required by a wolf pack.

In some ways, we can think about this in how companies are structured. Companies that are flat, i.e. less hierarchy, have fewer layers of management and tend to be more efficient than those with a taller hierarchical structure. This is because teams are more empowered and there are less bureaucratic restrictions on how to get the work done. Teams are more agile and tend to self-manage.

To summarize, take a look at the table below which compares the leadership traits required by both an organizational leader and a cheetah.

Organizational Leader vs. Cheetah

Strength Factors	Organizational Leader	Cheetah
Strategize	Recognize that one strategy does not fit all scenarios	Plans for optimal use of speed
Limitations	Using Multiple Distribution Channels versus a Single Channel to optimize growth.	Recognize that speed alone cannot lead to success. Other skills such as stealth and tracking are equally important.

CHAPTER 3

LEADING LIKE GIRAFFES

In the previous two chapters, we looked at animals that are considered predators in the wild. But predators are not the only leaders in the animal kingdom.

Let's take the giraffes, for example. They are plant-eaters. Giraffes demonstrate that you do not need to be aggressive to be a leader. Their skills and approach may be different from that of the predators, but those skills help them and their young stay safe. Three of the main characteristics that give giraffes an advantage are height, camouflage and strength.

These traits come into play when they try to get the upper hand against predators:

- Perceive danger early and warn the rest of the giraffes – Leveraging their height to increase their surveillance perimeter.

- Understand and protect themselves from potential risks – Using their natural camouflage in times of imminent danger.
- Confront adversity without fear - Using their strength to fight off predators if they get too close.
- Strength in numbers - Forming coalitions to protect their young.

These strengths play a big part in their survival in the wild. The same traits can also apply in an organizational setting.

Vigilance and Risk Assessment

A giraffe's height, along with its strong vision, allows it to see danger approaching from a distance. This allows a group of giraffes to react and protect themselves in time. They need to make split second decisions by determining if the animals in the vicinity are a threat, and then warn the herd accordingly.

Similarly, it is the responsibility of a leader in any organization to look out for the well-being of their employees and company. These leaders need to make good decisions that are in the best interests of the organization as a whole. This involves the ability to stay aware of the conditions in the marketplace or industry and decide on the next favorable move for the company.

The decisions made need to be evaluated in terms of the risk and potential impact to the company. Some decisions may involve more risk, but if the benefits outweigh the risk, then it is something the leader may deem worthwhile.

CHAPTER 3

Courage

Giraffes may not be predators but they have the ability to fight them off. Their strong hind legs are often used to deliver powerful blows to these predators. They bravely do this to protect themselves and their young.

A leader at any level in an organization needs to be strong. They need to be able to back up their decisions, stand up for their teams, and provide direction and confidence to the people in the organization. All these aspects require courage. Being passive or hesitant about "ruffling a few feathers" are traits of a poor leader.

Bringing a group together (for a common purpose)

Giraffes are said to be a "Fission-Fusion" society. This means they function independently of each other, but can come together when needed. Giraffe mothers usually form a nursery-type coalition to take care of their young together. Even with this type of defense, it is said that only about twenty-five percent of young giraffes make it to adulthood. The young are heavily targeted because they have less endurance and strength.

In an organization, it is the responsibility of a leader to bring together the right people for a particular purpose. This involves identifying people with the correct skills and abilities, and those that would be up for the task. The responsibility of coordinating and aligning everyone to a common goal lies with the leader. Additionally, they have to identify the team strengths, skill gaps, and how to address those.

Factors beyond the giraffe's control

Giraffes also have factors that pose a risk to their existence. These risks are primarily due to human interference and encroachment. This has resulted in the dwindling of the giraffe population. These are being addressed by creating awareness to the problem and the involvement of conservation groups to mitigate and remediate the situation.

Organizational leaders similarly face uncertainty and risks. They often have to plan for those unknowns by putting a mitigation plan in place. This sometimes includes outsourcing certain activities to shift or limit the risk to the organization.

To summarize, take a look at the table below which compares the leadership traits required by both an organizational leader and a giraffe.

CHAPTER 3

Organizational Leader vs. Giraffe

Strength Factors	Organizational Leader	Giraffe
Vigilant	Being aware of current market conditions and assess changes/ adjustments needed	Uses its height and vision to detect danger early and alert the herd
Courage	Has a fearless and confident approach to problem solving	Bravely stands up to predators and puts up a fight when required
Gain Alignment	Unites people with the required skills to drive towards a common goal	Come together for specific purposes e.g. taking care of young

SECTION 2

Lead That Thing! - Start with You

Now that we've seen what leadership entails and how it plays out in the animal kingdom, it is time to look at ourselves. If you are an aspiring leader, are you ready to lead?

Unlike animals, human leaders need one additional requirement - the correct mindset. This is often referred to as "Self-Leadership". Without self-awareness, humility or compassion, leaders are unlikely to be successful.

This section provides a survey, of sorts, that leaders or aspiring leaders should take to truly understand which aspects of leadership they are good at and which ones they can further develop. It provides examples of leaders in various settings and ties their abilities back to the subject areas addressed in the survey.

CHAPTER 4

ASSESS YOUR COMFORT LEVEL

Would you have ever thought that animals could give us insight into how to be better leaders?

In the previous chapters, we saw some of the leadership traits displayed by the wolf, cheetah, and giraffe and how we could incorporate those traits in an organization. Let's take a look at a few traits that a good leader would need.

Making Decisions (and saying "No")

Leadership involves making decisions. Even if leaders utilize a data-driven decision model, they may be forced to make decisions that are unpopular with their teams or peers e.g. when their final decision is in conflict with the opinions of the team. Consensus can be good in some situations, but a leader cannot always wait for consensus to drive efforts forward.

A leader mustn't be fixated on being popular. It is impossible to be liked by everyone. In life, we look to be our best based on how we treat ourselves and others. Likewise, companies and their leaders look to do good for their company, employees, and their customers. Along the way, there will be people that do not align with your goals, and that is something you need to be comfortable with instead of taking it personally.

Working horizontally and vertically (with peers and leaders)

As a leader, you will be expected to provide information or direction to either your peers or your superiors. This requires confidence and good communication skills. It is important to understand that the amount of details will vary with each group.

Communicating vertically to superiors and executives demands a more concise and specific message which they can use to draw insights on the company performance and make decisions accordingly.

Presenting information horizontally to peers, on the other hand, requires more detail. This is because peers need that detail to effectively support you and your teams.

Delegation

Whether it is running a home, school, company, or business, it is generally not possible for one person to do everything. Unless the scope of work involved in any of these entities is minimal, there will be a need for division of duties. Without this there would be overloading and eventual burnout.

CHAPTER 4

A leader needs to be comfortable with letting go of control and assigning work to others by providing clear expectations of outcomes. This frees up the leader to focus on more strategic matters and also develops more high performing individuals and teams.

A confident leader would not see the delegation as a threat, but rather as a duty to provide more people opportunities to lead and grow. This builds trust and loyalty and helps retain talent.

Deferring to the experts

Leaders cannot be experts in every single topic, but they need to have a good understanding of their business and industry. To gain knowledge on specific topics, however, they need to talk to experts and leverage their expertise when required. It would be foolish for a leader to pose as an expert on a subject when there are others with a vast amount of experience on exactly that topic. Leaders that know when and how to leverage their in-house experts do not see these experts as a threat to their position as a leader. Instead, they take pride in knowing their organization has the right talent to help achieve its goals.

Giving credit to others

When a project is successful, do you praise your team for generating that positive outcome? Or do you feel that your leadership was the bigger reason for the team's success? In most cases, success is a combination of both factors. Good leaders do not thrive on their ability to lead, but rather, on the success of their teams. Leadership should bring out the best in teams and should always keep team morale at a good point.

Leaders that struggle to give credit to the teams generally have insecurities about their ability to lead. They fear that the team may be seen as self-sufficient and reduce the leader's value in the organization. This is not something a true leader would be concerned about. Strong leaders constantly look out for the team's success and give credit where credit is due.

Owning your mistakes

Have you ever worked with a leader that could never admit they were wrong? This can play out in a few ways:

- They throw their team under the bus for their bad decisions
- They defend their decision despite all the facts against it
- They are unable to admit that they could have done better

This type of behavior does not help the leader, the team, or the company!

I have worked with a few leaders with this flaw and it is nothing less than aggravating. As a leader myself, I have seen that owning a mistake and focusing on what could be done differently in the future has helped me become a better and trusted leader. As a leader, I am not there to pose as though I know everything and can make no mistake. That is unrealistic and pretentious. It would also prevent my teams, peers and superiors from seeing me for my true abilities as a leader.

CHAPTER 4

Leadership Survey

Take some time to look at the factors discussed above and see where your comfort level lies on each of those points. Use a scale as shown below for each factor to determine your leadership baseline. This can help you easily identify whether you are ready to be a leader, or which behaviors you need to tweak (or which to acquire training for) to become a better leader.

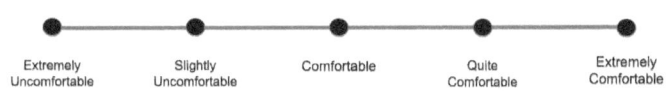

Where to start

To become a better leader, you have to start with yourself. Developing the right mindset and temperament is the first step to being successful. Leadership is about bringing out the best in people. This means that you, as a leader, must learn to focus on how you can help others thrive to have success as a whole.

There are many opportunities, beyond organizations, where we can be leaders. The next few chapters dive further into these scenarios with examples of leaders in action.

CHAPTER 5

AT WORK

Any work setting, be it corporate, start up, small business or non-profit, requires a leader to be successful.

The key duties of leaders in this setting are:

- Define the vision and goals of the organization
- Set expectations on the culture
- Select the people needed to achieve the vision
- Help individuals grow into leaders themselves
- Bring ideas to improve operations

Although the first two points above might be done by a senior leader or founder of the organization, the rest of the duties can be done by anyone, regardless of rank or title.

Let's look at Anya, a leader in the workplace, and how she fares with the Leadership survey.

Being a Leader at Work

Anya is the Director of Innovation in a small insurance company. She oversees a few teams and reports to the Chief Operations Officer. As the Director of Innovation, she has to research and elicit ideas about the company's evolution and competitiveness. This involves working with a diverse set of people inside and outside the company.

Making Decisions (and saying "No")

Leaders are often tasked with making the final decision on behalf of their team, department or organization. Anya most definitely cannot make this decision in a vacuum. She has to consult with in-house experts and sometimes, industry experts to arrive at a final decision on certain ideas. These decisions are not always unanimous. She has to be comfortable turning down certain ideas that do not align with the overall company strategy or those that pose financial or other risks. Anya also ensures that when she does turn down ideas, she backs her decision up with facts and reasoning. This helps people see her as trustworthy and respectful.

Working horizontally and vertically (with peers and leaders)

Whether you are a team leader or a CEO, you will always have to work with your peers, teams and leaders. Anya also has to work cross-organizationally to complete her innovation initiatives. She has to run the initial ideas for innovation by her boss to get alignment from a organizational standpoint, assess the teams she would need, and then direct the teams on their next steps. When there are dependencies on cross-functional teams, she has to talk to her peers to ensure that their teams' timelines align with hers.

Delegation

Once Anya gets the approvals and teams in place, her involvement is more of a servant-leader from that point on. In other words, she has to be there to guide and help the team if they have obstacles of some sort. Otherwise, she has to trust the team to complete their work. Having a consistent way of getting timely updates on the progress of the team helps her to have a finger on the pulse of the team without micro-managing them.

Deferring to the experts

Although Anya leads the company strategy around innovation, she needs the help of both the business and technical experts to form a fully-thought out plan. The insights and advice of these experts can help her determine the feasibility of an option or give her a better picture of the risk associated with any idea.

Giving credit to others

In line with a true leader, Anya makes it one of her top priorities to encourage teams to come up with ideas for innovation. Empowering teams to take ownership of their work allows them to come up with ideas to improve the status quo either from a process or a technology stand-point.

Anya always makes it a point to give credit to the idea owner. She believes this not only encourages more ideas, but it also helps people feel like they are in a position to lead change.

Owning your mistakes

To be successful in the world of "Innovation", it is important to have a mindset of experimentation, i.e. try something, observe the results, refine and redo until the desired outcome is achieved. Anya always insists on not being afraid of failure, since she truly believes that every so-called failure provides a lot of useful information to fuel the next iteration of the idea's implementation.

If an idea does not yield the necessary results, Anya takes ownership of that situation to provide the necessary updates to leaders and her peers. Since she directs the teams, she is also accountable for the outcomes of her teams. She takes on the task of explaining why an idea did not work and the steps being taken to refine the idea to achieve the expected results.

CHAPTER 6

IN THE COMMUNITY

Communities can be based on place of residence, ethnic backgrounds, interests, and generally any reason that brings people together because of shared experiences, or values.

For communities to be successful, they need leaders who can shepherd the activities of that community towards a shared vision.

The community leaders generally possess certain qualities:

- Bring people together
- Build relationships outside of the community
- Set direction and standards for the community
- Understand and act on the needs of the community

This requires them to lead, influence, negotiate, and communicate while being aware of the voice of the community.

Being a Leader in the Community

Misha is a leading member of her temple. Her duties include facilitating meetings about plans for community events, fund-raising and special prayers. She finds this aspect fulfilling and her communication and organizational skills helps her execute plans with perfection.

Making Decisions (and saying "No")

As with any community, there are many viewpoints, opinions, and wishes that cannot always be accommodated. Misha has to balance the needs of the temple with ideas from the larger community. Although all ideas from her community are well-intentioned, not all can be implemented. Misha has to carefully vet these ideas with other leaders in the community, weigh the overall benefit, and then decide whether to move forward or not. She also has to make sure that the members with ideas that are not selected, are kept in the loop and are called upon to help with implementing some of the selected ideas. This is a way Misha recognizes leadership within her community.

Working horizontally and vertically (with peers and leaders)

Misha has to acquire approvals from the city, or from temple board members for certain events she is coordinating. She then gets volunteers to pull the event together. This requires her to be seen as approachable and relatable, but also a leader in the eyes of the temple and the organizations with whom they partner.

Delegation

As dynamic as Misha is, she cannot organize events or set up programs within the temple without the help of volunteers and other people with the appropriate skills.

She has to trust people to be accountable and reliable and often vets them by building a relationship with them to understand their strengths, interests, and versatility. Pairing them with the appropriate job helps gain better results.

Deferring to the experts

Having built relationships, Misha understood who could help her with specific tasks. For example, some members are good at running the food service aspect, others are good at cultural presentations, and others specifically know what elements are needed for certain religious events. She turns to them to either run with certain tasks or gets their input on what is needed so she can get the necessary resources in place.

Giving credit to others

A community is nothing without its members. It is the synergy of all members that helps a community create its intended impact for its members.

Misha is diligent about promoting and awarding all the people that contribute towards making a change or event happen for the temple. This increases the well-being of the community as a whole and keeps people motivated.

Owning your mistakes

Being a community leader is a great responsibility. The main behavior that makes Misha a great community leader is not presenting herself as a "know-it-all". She is always receptive to feedback from the members of the community. Acknowledging her mistakes and this type of feedback is in the best interest of the community, its growth, and its health. The key here is that Misha does not think of the feedback as a personal dig but rather as an opportunity to improve both her effectiveness as a leader and the value provided to the community.

CHAPTER 7

AT HOME

For a home to run efficiently there needs to be some level of structure. Without that, there would be nothing but chaos, confusion and stress.

A home can have many different compositions. Here are a few examples:

- Parents and children
- Grandparents, parents and children
- A couple
- A Bachelor/Bachelorette

In each of these scenarios, there is a need for leadership. The example below further examines the challenges and demands of a leader at home.

Being a Leader at Home

Jay and Maya are the parents of a tween and a teen. In their experience, each of these phases requires a lot of tact, patience and assertiveness at times. Like many leaders, they need to possess some of the skills or traits mentioned in the previous chapter such as making decisions, delegating, owning their mistakes and so on.

Let's see how each of those traits applies to Jay and Maya's leadership journey at home.

Making Decisions (and saying "No")

The teen and tween phases can be a little tricky to navigate. This is when children start to get more independent and opinionated. We, as parents, should encourage these behaviors since this will help them be more successful in the long run. However, we need to carefully assess situations and be comfortable saying "No" and be ready to face the drama or music that ensues.

One day, their teen decided he didn't need to prepare for exams and wanted to spend time with friends and watch movies instead. This was an indication that Jay and Maya needed to step in and provide guidance. They realized they might be met with defiance, silence or a know-it-all attitude, but that is to be expected given the hormonal nature of teenagers. Jay and Maya knew not to take this personally, but rather lay out some structure for him e.g. "Spend X hours studying before you watch TV or spend time with your friends." It would lay some guard rails to help him stay on track.

The reality is that teenagers still have some growing up to do both physically and emotionally. This fact is backed up by many scientific studies of the teenage brain. The limbic system, which controls risk-reward and impulsive behaviors, develops much faster than the frontal lobe, which controls functions such as problem-solving and decision making. The result of this is more rash and careless decisions.

Parents like Jay and Maya have to put on that empathetic hat and work with these teens and tweens to solve problems or get them to do certain tasks.

Working horizontally and vertically (with peers and leaders)

Parents need to make sure they are in sync in terms of decision making. Children are quick to pick up on discrepancies between parents' point-of-views and can use this to their advantage. I can vouch for this from first-hand experience!

Jay and Maya have slightly different approaches to parenting. Maya often finds herself in the position of "Bad Cop". This forces her to proactively talk to Jay and ensure that they present themselves as a united front to the kids. Maya recognizes the importance of communication, transparency and expectations setting.

Once Maya aligns with Jay on the direction for the kids, she communicates her message to the kids. Since both parents are on the same page, the kids cannot find loopholes. Maya also ensures that she doesn't talk to the kids in a patronizing manner. This tone of voice would only make the children more resistant to her advice.

Delegation

Mothers like Maya often make the mistake of feeling as though they need to take care of everything. This often comes from the need to be in control. That is not necessarily a bad thing, but should be balanced with allowing others to learn and grow.

One particular task Maya is a stickler about is loading the dishwasher. She is very particular about how to efficiently place the plates and bowls so that more dishes can fit in a single load. She often wants to just take care of this task on her own.

What Maya has to force herself to do is to clearly communicate her concerns or even demonstrate better ways to load the dishwasher. If she plays that coach, she can teach her kids some basic life skills as well as have people to help her with that task and focus on other important household or professional duties.

Deferring to the experts

As parents, we think we are experts in all subjects when compared to our children, right? However, there are some situations where we need to talk to our spouses, educational advisors, financial advisors or home improvement advisors to take care of matters concerning our homes, finances or kids.

Jay and Maya, for example, consult with financial advisors to manage their finances and investments to ensure a good future for their family.

CHAPTER 7

Giving credit to others

Couples inevitably have different skill sets. This is what makes them a good team. Just as a team deserves credit when they do a good job, couples have to acknowledge each other and their children when they come up with ideas or solve problems for the family.

Jay and Maya have a healthy relationship and constantly show gratitude towards each other and to their kids. Jay and Maya especially make it a point to give credit to the teachers that help their kids persist and succeed in activities like music and sports.

Parental involvement is key, for sure, but their partners or allies shape their kids' experiences to make them more well-rounded. Giving credit to the teachers shows that the parents are very secure in their role and are also very comfortable in being in a support role for some of the activities.

Owning your mistakes

As a parent, I try to stay level-headed, but it is not always possible. Especially in situations where there is a lack of cooperation from either my children or my spouse. In these situations, I sometimes lose my composure. This is almost always followed by regret.

Jay and Maya face problems or conflicts at times. The complexity of these matters range from something as simple as who has to take the trash out to determining the schools and activities their kids should attend. Sometimes their work stresses make them less tolerant and they aren't in control of their emotions.

The key to recovery for both of them is to admit they have been short with each other or the kids and help explain their point of view so that the person on the receiving end can understand it isn't meant to be taken personally. They also reflect on how they can better handle similar matters in the future.

CHAPTER 8

AT SCHOOL

Having observed my children from elementary through high school, I can confidently say that kids start to discover their ability to lead as early as elementary school. Sometimes it takes the form of being "bossy", but at that age, being bossy can also be interpreted as being confident enough to take the lead.

Some kids are more passive during elementary school and middle school but then go on to find their voice in high school. Leadership in high school looks very different from that seen in elementary school. High schoolers cannot get away with being "bossy" due to push back from their peers. Leaders here take more initiative and are skilled at delegating and creating ownership within others.

There are different opportunities for leadership at each level of school. Here are some examples:

Elementary School - Group competitions and projects bring out leaders to coordinate, divide and complete the work.

Middle School - Students have an opportunity to mentor kids in elementary school. Additionally, heading up and running student clubs or participating in national competitions grows leadership in these students.

High School - Sports captains, band section leaders and club founders are all examples of positions in which students can exercise and utilize their leadership skills. This sometimes results in them being role models or the go-to person for their peers.

Let's look at a leader in middle school in relation to the Leadership survey.

Being a Leader at School

Sam is a seventh grader. He is a hard-working student and is involved with the Yearbook club and the school's Cross-country team. He is very outgoing and is always looking to get people involved in activities for and around the school. He is very well liked by his peers and teachers.

Making Decisions (and saying "No")

As an essential member of the year book club, Sam has to ensure that members are engaged in its activities. He has to recognize when the head of the club needs help with coordinating and running its initiatives.

Many times, in a club with ten to twenty members, there will be differing opinions. For initiatives that Sam is put in charge of he has to be comfortable saying "No" to certain suggestions if they don't align either from a cost or resource perspective. It is tough to say "No" because it can potentially cause a person to lose interest in the club, but Sam does it with tact and encourages open conversations on how that idea could be implemented within the budget and timeline of the club and school.

Working horizontally and vertically (with peers and leaders)

To start or run a club, it is very important to have the support of teachers. Having their support can help grow the club and create more opportunities because of the reach and influence of the teachers.

Sam has to often bring his ideas for the club to his teachers to get official approval. This requires him to be comfortable talking to them and lay out his case with all the supporting justification. Additionally, he has to be very clear in his communication with the rest of the club.

Delegation

A club needs all its members to participate to get its goals accomplished. This task cannot be handled by a single person or a small group of people. That would not only be inefficient, it would be counter-intuitive to the purpose of the club which is to provide an opportunity for students to lead in their capacities.

Sam, as one of the leaders, has to understand the members' strengths and interests to appropriately assign groups or tasks to each of them.

Deferring to the experts

In every club, there will be a pool of talent. In the yearbook club, some may be good at photography, others at writing, and some at editing or designing.

Sam has to pay attention to the experts in these arenas and make sure to engage them when decisions have to be made relating to those topics. If Sam and the other leaders of the club make the decisions in a vacuum, that would be an uneducated decision and would demean the presence of the experts.

Having the expert weigh in helps ensure all the necessary details are accounted for before arriving at a final decision.

Giving credit to others

A yearbook, for example, is the work of a group and not a single individual. Sam and the rest of the club leaders always make it a point to call out members that help out with tasks for the club. This not only makes that member feel good, but it also creates a positive team culture.

Sam even highlights any outstanding work done by members every week to keep people motivated.

Owning your mistakes

Sam, for his age, is very level-headed and has high emotional intelligence.

The pressure of school occasionally makes him a little less patient with others. This is a rare occurrence, but when it does happen, Sam catches it right away, acknowledges it, and makes sure to keep those stresses

CHAPTER 8

out of the interactions. Sometimes he has a one-on-one with the person to apologize for his impertinence.

SECTION 3

Lead That Thing! With Integrity and Grit

The previous section showed us some different perspectives of leadership in daily life. It demonstrated how leaders in any context require the same basic skills.

This section dives deeper into the definition of Leadership. It starts by clearing up common misconceptions about leadership and how leadership extends beyond "titles".

CHAPTER 9

LEADERSHIP... WHAT IT IS NOT!

Leadership is still a relatively subjective term. Its definition varies by culture, industry, and occupation.

Some forms of "leadership" are nothing more than toxic and unhealthy for the people being subjected to that agony. A recent study by DDI, a Leadership Consulting firm, revealed that about 57 percent of employees left their job due to a bad manager. Luckily, there are also more forward-thinking styles of leadership where people's morale and motivation stay intact and are more often elevated.

Having worked in the technology field for more than fifteen years, I have seen my fair share of good leaders and not-so-good leaders. I learned a lot from both types. I have developed and adjusted my leadership style based on observations of these leaders. The good leaders inspired me to be a stronger leader and the bad leaders made me aware of behaviors I wanted to completely avoid.

Throughout my career, I have seen a few flavors of leadership gone wrong.

1. Get stuff done at any "cost"
2. Leadership fueled by insecurities
3. Passive and never challenges the status quo
4. Great technical expert, weak leader
5. Never questions/challenges the Executives' ideas

Let's look at each of these categories in detail.

Get stuff done at any "cost"

Some leaders feel their success is defined by how much they get their team to deliver. With this goal in mind, they sometimes lose sight of all the other factors that should be considered when running a project or organization. This includes things like maintaining a positive environment for their teams, allowing for a work-life balance, and building a healthy team dynamic through empowerment.

The consequences of this approach are the teams' lack of trust and respect for the leader.

Leadership fueled by insecurities

In my experience, both in and out of the workplace, I noticed that most overtly "bossy" people inevitably have some deep-rooted insecurities. They use this bossy facade as a way to protect themselves; it's a defense mechanism of sorts. Leaders with this issue are less likely to be open to ideas, tend to shut down ideas from others, and take things personally when people do not accept their ideas.

A combination of all those symptoms mentioned above makes the workplace an extremely undesirable place to be. This is how companies lose some very talented resources.

Passive and never challenges the status quo

I cringe whenever I hear a leader say, "That's the way we've always done it!" It is a red flag that indicates the leader is not open to change and is not comfortable challenging an outdated culture. As much as I hear the words, "Culture eats strategy for breakfast", I find it hard to believe that a true leader cannot influence that change.

I have witnessed dramatic changes in culture when a clear strategy is brought into play by the top executives. As long as a leader can devise a strategy that better positions a company in terms of growth and health, there is always hope for change. This message can then be trickled down to the various levels of the organization. The strategy becomes more of a requirement than an option. This is very likely to make a lot of people uncomfortable, but that is the nature of organizational change.

Leaders that simply sit back and don't even try to change visible dysfunction in an organization cannot genuinely call themselves leaders. I believe the apt word for them is "Enablers" since they allow a bad culture to propagate itself.

Great technical expert...weak leader

Have you ever watched the show "The Office"? The lead character, Michael Scott, plays a top salesman turned manager. He turns out to be a completely incompetent manager who doesn't garner any respect from most of his subordinates and has no clue how to professionally lead his branch. Although Michael is a fictional character, there is some truth to how his character is depicted.

Just because a person excels at their technical craft does not automatically imply that they possess the skills to be a leader; a mentor or coach, maybe, but not a leader. Companies often overlook this when they promote their resident experts into a leadership position. These experts turned leaders are unable to make decisions, challenge others, or back up the team in tough times. The company itself would be better off with them being in their technical role until they are coached, mentored and ready to be a leader.

Never Question/Challenge the Executives

Executives are very much in tune with the direction and strategies of the company. The success of a company starts with strong executives that are dynamic and fully aware of the changing market climates. It is rare for them to have a pulse on the day-to-day operations of the company. They depend on their direct reports and leaders on the ground to be transparent about risks and issues they foresee with work that is being done for the company.

Leaders who are more intent on scoring points with the executives than painting an accurate picture are doing a

CHAPTER 9

disservice to their executives, departments and teams. This behavior demonstrates a lack of backbone and inability to do the right thing for the company as a whole. This type of leader does not realize that the executives depend on them to be honest, and they expect those leaders to challenge them, when appropriate, rather than being robotic "Yes, (Wo)Men" or "Brown Nosers".

Have you had experiences with "leaders" with the characteristics discussed above? Hopefully, recognizing that these are faux leaders gives you renewed hope for your career journey and growth as a leader.

The next chapter covers the difference between a leader and a manager. These terms are used interchangeably, but there is a distinct difference.

CHAPTER 10

LEADERS vs. MANAGERS

Early on in my career I viewed leaders and managers as the same thing. As I progressed, I started to realize what traits distinguish a person as a leader as opposed to a manager. All leaders are managers to some extent, but not all managers are leaders as shown in the diagram below.

Managers vs. Leaders

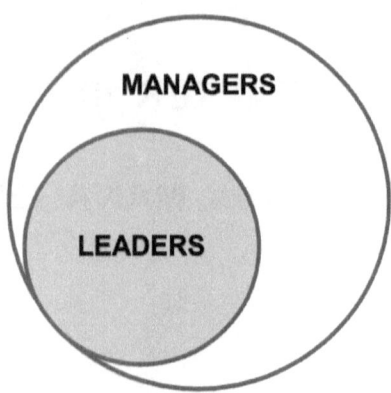

Leader

These are some traits associated with a Leader:

- Inspires teams
- Guides people
- Innovates by being willing to fail
- Gives credit where it's due

A leader's work is more strategic.

Manager

A Manager, on the other hand, has more defined duties:

- Ensures that the day-to-day work gets done on time
- Helps their team members set professional goals

CHAPTER 10

- Enables their team to have the resources needed to achieve those goals
- Evaluates their team's performance
- Protects the team from "noise" i.e. distractions that do not need to be imposed on the team

The Manager's duties are much more tactical and process-oriented.

Let's look at a scenario and distinguish how it is approached by both a manager and a leader.

How to Lead vs. Manage

AK Tech is a software development company within the Banking Industry. One of its teams, Team X is currently working on a high profile initiative that will change the consumer experience and make their company innovators in the industry. Team X is a high performing team with self-starters. The work for this initiative has been scoped out and the team is heads down in the execution phase.

While Team X is in the midst of their project, another request comes from one of the C-Level Executives. It is a strategic initiative that puts the company at par with other companies in the same industry. It has a very specific deadline with financial repercussions. The problem, however, is that it requires the skill set that is only available in Team X.

By the basics of Product and Project Management 101, it is obvious that if Team X has to take on this new initiative along with their current project, there would need to be some basic re-planning:

- Understand whether the team can take on the additional project without compromising the existing effort
- Determine if there are additional resources needed to help complete both projects
- Analyze the priorities within each initiative to optimize team efforts to align with the value delivered to the customer; shelve lower priority items
- Lay out a realistic plan that can accomplish leadership expectations

All these things are the responsibility of a manager. They coordinate and facilitate the conversations with all the people involved to get things in motion. A good manager is organized, assertive, and communicates effectively. They know whom to leverage and how to delegate.

Now, let's assume that after the planning, Team X determines that even with only the minimum essential components being done, the work would potentially be delivered a month beyond the deadline. In response, the C-Level executive restates there is no flexibility whatsoever in the deadline.

Your basic run-of-the-mill "manager" would probably work his or her team to the bone to get the work done since they feel their primary duty is to make the team meet their commitments. In some cultures or environments this may be viewed as a positive, and would perhaps even make the manager be perceived as "strong". In reality, this is not good management at all. It demoralizes the employees.

CHAPTER 10

A good manager, on the other hand, does have an opportunity to be a leader in this scenario.

- They can have a conversation with the executive and understand "why" the new effort needs to be done now and get a better picture of the true "value" of working on that initiative.
- They have to be transparent with the executive on not being able to realistically meet the deadline without any major changes to the scope of work.
- They can present some alternatives to the executive on how and when to do the work and what other pieces may need to shift as a result.

The above points are things that would be done by a leader. They are not afraid to question decisions from executives and are more willing to stand up for their team. Leaders always have the "big picture" in mind and are constantly thinking of how best to get sustainable results and growth for their team.

Both Leaders and Managers are undoubtedly important in an organization, but they each require a different mindset and skillset. As shown above, a manager can rise to the occasion and be a leader, but not all managers are leaders, or want to be leaders in the true sense of the word.

CHAPTER 11

INFLUENCE vs. AUTHORITY

Have you ever been in a situation where you wish you had the "authority" to direct a group of people to carry out your idea?

That type of "power", if used properly, comes in handy when you are a leader dealing with a disaster. But the "do as I say approach" doesn't build the trust and following you expect in the long run. It turns people away because they don't feel heard.

John R. P. French and Bertram H. Raven, Social psychologists, did a study in 1959 that found there are five forms of power:

1. **Coercive Power** - Ability to force someone to do what you ask

2. **Reward Power** - Ability to provide a reward for doing something that is not of interest to you or take away privileges for failing to do that task
3. **Legitimate Power** - Power to give direction based on the position in the organization
4. **Referent Power** - Ability to influence by being a representation of standards to which others can strive
5. **Expert Power** - Ability to influence by being a subject matter expert

The first three are related to holding a title that allows you to make decisions and have consequences for those who comply or don't comply. These types of power have more to do with "authority", as defined by the person's title or role.

The last two types of power, referent and expert, can be possessed by any person, at any level, in any role in an organization.

An Influential Case Study

Becky was recently hired as a software engineer for a Financial Institute. She brings a lot of knowledge and ideas to this organization from her diverse experience in a variety of companies and industries. Her team has five other engineers, a quality analyst, a team lead, a product manager and a resource manager. The resource manager is primarily responsible for the goals and growth of the team whereas the team lead assists with executing and monitoring the day-to-day activities of the team. The product manager works with the team to understand the

CHAPTER 11

customer needs and determines the priorities on which the team focuses their effort.

After a few weeks of working with the team, Becky realized there were some basic inefficiencies within the team. A lot of time was spent in rework, and deployments were a heavily manual process. She realized that the team had been functioning this way for a while and couldn't address the problem due to the constant demand on them.

Drawing from her experiences in other companies, she knew that taking some time to address the issues would help the team take on more work without compromising quality. Some ideas she wanted to propose were:

- Automation of testing whenever possible to save time and increase consistency
- Making the Product Manager the point-person for the customers to triage demands and ensure less disruption to the team
- Planning the team's work for shorter periods and right-sizing the deliveries to get faster feedback and reduce rework

As a software engineer, she did not have the "authority" per se to implement all these ideas. She needed to work with and talk to the people that could help get these plans in motion.

She would need more than just a narrative to convince the team and her leaders to introduce these changes, so she put some metrics together with some visuals depicting the benefits that would be gained.

She approached the Team Lead to share her thoughts and gain buy-in for her ideas. The Team Lead was receptive to the ideas knowing that the changes would improve not only the team's performance, but their morale as well. Together, they came up with a plan to communicate this to the leaders and explain the benefits. Becky knew that the leaders may be hesitant about dramatic change, so she made sure that the plan she proposed included options for addressing these changes in small increments. This would also give the team and its leaders a chance to see the improvements at a micro-level and feel comfortable in the decision to pursue that direction.

Becky was able to get these changes into motion within a short period. The key strategies that helped her do this were:

1. Formulate the idea - Use data and visuals to support the proposal.
2. Approach potential allies - Allies would be people with the authority to help you gather the right people.
3. Make it about experimentation - People are more willing to test smaller changes before committing to an overhaul of old habits. Big change is intimidating.

We often underestimate our ability to influence primarily because we feel we do not have the "power" to do so. If we get past that misconception, each of us can feel more empowered to bring our ideas forth and make a difference in our organizations. Being able to sell your idea and its potential benefits make you a leader!

SECTION 4

Lead That Thing! The Real World

This section concludes the book with successful real life leadership journeys!

I share my conversations with some leaders in the Milwaukee area, their career journeys, and advice for aspiring leaders.

CHAPTER 12

RICK PARKS

Rick Parks - CEO, Society Insurance

Leadership Journey

Rick found himself leading efforts right from high school. Whenever something needed to get done, people turned to Rick to take the lead. The question he asked himself often was "Do I add the most value in this role?" If the answer was "Yes", he took on the responsibility.

This pattern repeated itself through college and the business world. His attitude was not, "What's in it for me?" It was, "How can I help and add value to this organization?" Even in the corporate world, his drive was more related to finding opportunities to better an organization with his knowledge and experience rather than being focused on scaling the corporate ladder.

In challenging times, such as during Covid-19, he had one main approach to providing hope and optimism to the employees - Communication! Rick made it a point to communicate regularly with the employees and leaders in his organization.

He focused on transparency around:

- The challenges on the table
- The opportunities for change
- The areas of uncertainty
- The information available at a point in time

Rick states the three traits of a good leader are:

1. The desire to make a difference - having the intent to help others
2. Maintaining humility - not assuming you are better than the next person
3. Having an inquisitive mind - being well versed in your business and its dynamic, shifting needs

CHAPTER 13

D. HOLLY LIFKE

D. Holly Lifke - Chief Human Resources Officer and Executive Vice President, The Boldt Company

Holly always felt a deep responsibility to help people in need. This trait, combined with contagious energy and enthusiasm caused people to turn to her for help when they needed a strong leader. She attributes her ability to stay calm in a crisis to her mom, her mentor. Her mom taught her to be strong, independent, self-reliant, and adaptive. This helps her lead people with clarity in the toughest of situations.

A core part of her journey involved three things - learning, changing, and adapting.

Leadership Journey

Early in her career, when she was working at FDIC, she had the opportunity to lead examinations and teach. This made her realize what sparked her passion. It involved helping others by:

- Problem Solving
- Connecting the dots
- Enabling them to see the capabilities they didn't realize they had
- Laying out a plan for people to tap into their full potential

Her willingness to roll up her sleeves and get things done got her opportunities to challenge herself and grow as a leader. She summarizes her learnings over the years as follows:

- Leadership is an honor and responsibility - it is not about ego or self-gratification. It is about Servant Leadership.
- Her faith has given her the strength and skills to navigate difficult situations, help people through tough times, and give them hope and optimism for the future.
- The key is to know who you are and what you want - If she feels restless, she finds herself making BIG changes. Change gets her excited

because it is an opportunity to learn and address new challenges.
- Leadership style is important – This means being open and candid, sharing ideas, and synergizing. A leader should be willing to accept ideas from others and be able to admit ideas from others might be better
- There is plenty to go around. Focus on growing the pie, not dividing it up. Build something greater.
- Humility is a key trait. This means the willingness to say "I am wrong... I don't know...Teach me!" Leadership is not about having all the answers.
- Hiring a leader impacts the culture based on how they are wired to work in a place full of talented people.
- Building energized and trusting teams rather than stifling creativity helps establish a healthy culture where people can grow and be creative.

"Culture eats strategy for breakfast"

Holly believes culture should be "How" you execute your strategy. The two must be aligned.

She says a strong culture with a bad strategy can still get results, but they may not be optimal. A bad culture paired with a good strategy, on the other hand, will result in failure.

Culture is often used as an excuse not to execute on a strategy or make difficult decisions simply because it challenges the status quo. This behavior has to be addressed for a company to be successful.

Dealing with Social unrest and a Pandemic

In response to the recent social unrest, Holly notes that we all have an opportunity to influence even if we are not a "Leader" by title. She says it is important to recognize that we are all imperfect. We need to call each other out and have the courage to improve culture from a diversity and inclusion perspective by having open conversations on these topics. The key is to validate everyone, their journey and values.

Holly played a key role in coordinating the changes through the pandemic. Some of her primary areas of focus were serving as part of the team focusing on the health of her employees and the health of the business:

- Communication - keeping employees constantly informed of the changes and impact to the company.
- Safety of Employees - this involved daily communications and tracking of state-specific decisions.
- Work from Home transitions - allowing employees to make decisions based on their comfort levels in regards to staying home versus coming into the office, and providing tools to be successful and supportive through challenges.
- Supporting projects in meeting customer needs.

These things helped employees cope better with the changes and gave them a sense of trust in leadership.

CHAPTER 14

ANDY WEINS

Andy Weins - CEO, Green Up Solutions

Leadership - Nature vs. Nurture.

Andy considers himself a born leader. Growing up he was rebellious and always paved his own path. Whether it was getting his first job, moving out, or doing his own thing, he was the first in his circle to do these things.

He led by asking questions and always questioned the group-think mentally. His experience in the military, with its built-in structure, gave him an idea of "What right looked like". It brought change to how he approached leadership and management.

Manager vs. Leader

Andy says, "You lead people. You manage processes." He gives the example of managing and leading in a warehouse. Managers manage processes and inventory. Leaders empower, train, coach, and mentor to execute those processes.

Andy states:

- Leaders need to recognize the human psyche is always moving.
- Leaders support and encourage others to create an environment where everyone can figure things out together.
- Leaders do not do something solely because that's the way it's always been done. They challenge the status quo.

Transition within Military

Before the military, Andy says he was guilty of micromanaging. This continued in the military where he was able to get compliance, but wasn't "leading". His wake up call came when he was called out by squad leader Staff Sergeant Sanchez who he was overseeing.

Staff Sergeant Sanchez assertively and candidly stated that he needed more autonomy and that he wasn't getting this from Andy's style of leadership. This gave Andy food for thought. It was at this point that he decided to change his approach toward the people he led, paying more attention to what they needed from him and responding with more empathy and support. This change resulted in people being more drawn to him and accepting him as a leader.

Challenges

"You can have a perfect process and perfect system, but if no one follows it, it doesn't really matter!" he says, referring to an incident in Cuba.

While in Cuba, Andy saw a few things that were unethical and immoral. His reactions to his superiors in this scenario were not well received and resulted in his removal from the position. It was a rough period for him personally and professionally. Sergeant Sanchez, who then became his mentor, helped Andy understand that although he was right in pointing out things that were not morally correct, he needed to use a different approach to get this point of view heard. In retrospect, Andy learned that he needed to recraft his message in such a way that it became meaningful to those supervisors. In other words, what was in it for them and how could change benefit their organization. This would be more effective than a purely emotional outburst and protest.

He summarizes the experience in this way:

"Often the squeaky wheel gets the grease, but in this case, it got replaced, because it was affecting overall performance."

Entrepreneur

Andy's experience as a leader also extends to Entrepreneurship. His company, Green Up Solutions, uses UV light technology and an antimicrobial solution to provide hospital grade protection and disinfection to everyday environments. The organization serves facilities like senior living, daycares, manufacturing, schools, gyms, etc.

At the onset of Covid-19, he realized how unprepared his organization was because of the extent to which these services were needed. Initially, he had to lay off several employees because all businesses were closed for an extended period. When it came time to start rehiring, he made more intentional decisions around the employees he would bring back. He saw this as an opportunity to reset his organization to have people with the right mindsets and work ethic that would support his vision and cause.

Advice to Aspiring leaders

Andy's motivational phrase for aspiring leaders is, "Do the f*ing thing!" He encourages people to do it their own way with a focus on results. He says this will guide their path.

Culture - Organizations vs. Organisms

When thinking about organizational culture, Andy draws an analogy with an organism as shown below.

CHAPTER 14

Function	Organism	Organization
Growth and Characteristics	Determined by the organism's nucleus and DNA	Determined by the organization's people and cultural norms
Keeping it moving	The cytoplasm contains all the elements that help the organism function efficiently	Strategy and processes help organizations reach their goals and be successful
Protecting from harm	The cell membrane controls what comes in and goes out. It is the responsibility of the whole cell to fight toxicity	Human Resources, Managers, and team mates have to take the appropriate actions to reduce the effect of toxic employees

A new hire has an opportunity to impact the culture in an organization much like a new element in an organism causes a change or reaction in an organism. New people will bring in new norms. Entertaining their ideas around culture helps make them feel valued versus managed.

In the event of toxicity, the onus is on the entire organism or organization to get rid of the "toxic" object or behavior.

CHAPTER 15

RASHI KHOSLA

Rashi Khosla - CEO, MARS Solutions Group

Leadership Journey

Rashi considers herself an "accidental" entrepreneur. The need to spend more time with her kids made her go down the entrepreneurship path which gave her more flexibility than she had with her corporate job. The need for work-life balance and family values was what drove the culture and drew people to her company. She wanted the company to have intentional, sustainable, and meaningful growth.

Fears

Rashi's biggest fear was to leave her corporate job and take on entrepreneurship full time. She overcame that fear by diving into the business and letting her experience as a leader guide her. She also reached out to mentors, family, and other leaders. Their support made her feel that she couldn't fail. Being a lifelong learner, she dove deep into the elements of her business.

"Fear can either get you or can drive you!" she says. Since Rashi's household was not solely dependent on her income she thought, "Why not do it?!" She felt the biggest fear was putting herself out there. Rashi encountered Imposter Syndrome many times during this journey and learned to be aware of it and reel it back to keep from succumbing to it.

Challenges

Rashi's biggest challenge at the onset of her business was finding her first client. As a woman, and one with a diverse background, she had to work harder than others to claim her executive presence and to feel like she belonged.

She had to let her work speak for itself. Her drive eventually led to her success making others see her as a leader.

Dealing with a Pandemic

Two priorities Rashi focused on during Covid-19 were:

1. Employee engagement
2. Employee safety

She intentionally showed vulnerability by sharing her life at home, during video calls, so others could be comfortable doing the same.

She worked with HR to arrange activities for weekly engagement to keep morale up and ensured that employees were taking time off. She also implemented a way to create weekly goals for employees to keep them motivated and rewarded them for their achievements.

When it came time to start getting employees back into the office, the plan was driven by the employees (their choice) and structured by HR so that everyone's comfort level and convenience were accounted for. Rashi says that the organization was functioning so well in the remote environment that she had no concerns about people taking their time to come back into the physical office. She felt comfortable empowering them to make that decision for themselves.

Giving back to the community

Rashi gives back to the community in many ways - Tech Coalition and Returnship are two of her latest ventures.

Tech Coalition is an effort by local Milwaukee companies to attract tech talent from across the nation to start making Milwaukee more of a Tech Hub.

As part of this initiative, she has also been helping women get back to work - coaching them and putting them in front of hiring managers. She refers to this project as "MARS Returnship". The MARS Returnship program is an on-ramp for women looking to restart their careers in technology following a gap in employment. She provides on-the-job training, mentorship, and a partnership approach to prepare women to successfully rejoin the workforce. The program looks to provide high-caliber, female technical talent to employers that value gender diversity and inclusion.

Additionally, Rashi serves on the board of Ronald McDonald House of Changes and is on the Committee for I.C. Stars and Neolink.

CHAPTER 16

BRENDA CAMPBELL

Brenda Campbell - CEO, Secure Futures

Leadership Journey

Brenda had a background in Social Work and started by evaluating child welfare programs. This job came with lots of bureaucracy and red tape. She often took a problem, came up with solutions and presented them to leadership but, more often than not, she could not make progress due to the hierarchical structure and budgetary limitations of the organization. This was very frustrating to her and she felt that she could no longer make a difference in that organization.

Brenda was sharing this frustration with a friend one day who then directed her to an individual looking to start an organization to help teens with financial literacy. At first, she felt she had no experience working in financial education, no fundraising experience, and had never led a nonprofit organization. She wasn't sure how she could lead without that knowledge, but she realized that her strength was in building programs and this was the skill set that was needed. She used her program background to develop the organization from the ground up, and put a program structure in place that has allowed the organization to serve more than 85,000 teens over the past fourteen years.

Challenges

When she first took on the leadership role at SecureFutures, Brenda found herself falling victim to Imposter Syndrome. She often second-guessed her decisions, but with time, she learned that her instincts were spot on. Her confidence grew and her advice and perspective is now sought after by nonprofit and business leaders.

Brenda notes that she understood the mission of the organization because her family was not well-to-do and she was a first-generation college graduate. She understood how this education could help children because she would have benefitted from it in her teen years. The mission resonated very closely with her.

CHAPTER 16

Serving the Clients

Milwaukee Public Schools (MPS) was the first partner for SecureFutures. In the early years, and with a staff of two, Brenda wore all the hats in the organization. She was responsible for recruiting, training, and managing volunteers. She also developed curriculum-recruited board members, and raised every dollar needed to support the programming.

Since this was her first experience as a nonprofit leader, Brenda surrounded herself with experienced leaders to guide her in all aspects of nonprofit leadership and fundraising. She leveraged networking to find these experts and gained knowledge through these interactions.

She also faced the challenge of being the only woman in the early board meetings. This was something she had to tolerate, but then worked to get a stronger and more diverse representation on the board. She sought out people that represented the communities being served, and then hired the right talent needed for the organization. This resulted in more empowerment and respect across the organization and the board.

Brenda uses a data-informed approach to curriculum and program development. She created a structure that allows for continuous feedback from students, educators and volunteers. That, combined with behavioral-focused outcomes, is used to continuously enhance the program and sets SecureFutures apart from other organizations focused on financial education.

Covid-19

With the onset of Covid-19, the SecureFutures program team had to make a quick shift to virtual learning. This was relatively new territory. As schools shut down, some programs had to be canceled. The first priority was to provide guidance, accounting for various styles of distance learning, to help teachers in a virtual setting. SecureFutures' innovative Money Path program, an app-based technology designed to help students connect the dots between their career/college plans and their financial futures, has been an especially useful resource in the virtual learning environment.

Social Unrest

Brenda sees silence as a sign of complacency and acceptance, and believes we all need to speak up in the face of injustice. The social climate has enabled the organization to have open conversations and show support for their colleagues and clients who are directly impacted by racial inequity. The SecureFutures team is ready to double down on their efforts to work on equity and financial inclusion.

CHAPTER 17

BILL BUNZEL

Bill Bunzel - Vice President - Property and Liability Insurance, Society Insurance

Leadership Journey

Bill does not consider himself a "natural leader". He gives credit to his coaches for making him the leader he is today.

Early on, as a leader, he thought he had to be the smartest person in the room. Then he started to realize there was a lot to be learned from listening and speaking last. He realized that the people who surrounded him had the answers and he learned to embrace that and support them.

He says he was an awful leader in the beginning. His style was to improve people's performances by pointing out their mistakes and faults.

With time, he learned that this approach wasn't ideal. He wasn't getting the results he desired and the employees were not happy either. This made him change his approach:

- He started to provide positive reinforcement and help people build on their strengths.
- He learned to build their trust and confidence such that they started to do things for themselves which is the best reward for a leader.
- He stretched them to do things.

Bill, like Rashi and Brenda, often experienced Imposter Syndrome because he found himself in positions where he was not necessarily the expert. The way he had to overcome that feeling was to:

- Be open and vulnerable about short-comings
- Acknowledge the expertise of the people in the teams

Challenges

Bill states that one of his biggest challenges was not seeing the big picture. He had to learn about all parts of the organization and not just be department focused. Once he understood the importance of having a broader perspective, he made it a point to provide his staff with the opportunity to learn about other departments. This resulted in them growing and contributing to more than just their assigned department, giving them job satisfaction.

Advice for Aspiring leaders

Bill has the following advice for aspiring leaders:

- Learn about the other parts of your organization - understand the big picture and make connections across the organization. This opens up opportunities for growth.
- Get mentors and coaches to guide you - having coaches outside of your department or organization will help you build a broader perspective on how to lead in your context.

Dealing with a Pandemic

The role of communication became even more important during the pandemic. Bill sent out weekly updates and messages to his staff. He specifically tried to guide them to take care of themselves and seek out support to get through the uncertain and tough period.

He sees his employees as "the most important asset in the company". By keeping them in good health, he believes they can, in turn, provide the best service for customers.

EPILOGUE

Leadership exists in many contexts. We've seen leadership in animals, at work, in the home and more. Leaders guide, teach, and help others grow.

A world without leadership keeps us static and will likely result in a decline in the overall health of our societies and communities. Each of us can be leaders, whether we have a "title" or not. We all have the power to positively influence the direction in which our organizations and communities are moving, so why not?

A great leader can be characterized by 3Cs - **Confidence**, **Compassion**, and **Curiosity**.

Confidence - Having a sense of direction and not having a "fear of failure".

Compassion - Empathizing with co-workers, customers, or employees to consider their best interests.

Curiosity - Always wanting to learn. The world is constantly changing and therefore needs are constantly changing. A leader has to stay on top of these changes to effectively strategize solutions for the problems at bay.

The Leadership Survey included in Chapter 4 and the 3Cs above are great tools to gauge your progress as a leader.

Enjoy your leadership journey!

ABOUT THE AUTHOR

Aruna Krishnan is a Business Strategy Consultant, Best Selling Author, and Podcast Host. Her "Busy Mind" book series and Podcast "Lead That Thing!" cover leadership topics and competencies.

She also has 15+ years of experience in the Technology field and leads efforts to define, design and deliver high quality products for customers.

Aruna's main mission in life is to lift up people and help them find happiness and success by encouraging them through content, stories and inspiration!

She can be reached on Instagram or Facebook.

@leadthatthing

OTHER BOOKS BY ARUNA KRISHNAN

Available on Amazon

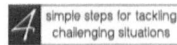

Aruna Krishnan

Available on Amazon

LOOKING FOR MORE ON LEADERSHIP?

LISTEN TO LEAD THAT THING!

A Podcast by Aruna Krishnan

Available on **Google Podcasts**, **Apple Podcasts** and **Spotify**

A NOTE FROM THE AUTHOR

Thank you for taking the time to read my book. I would greatly appreciate it if you would leave me an honest review on Goodreads or Amazon.

www.ingramcontent.com/pod-product-compliance
Lightning Source LLC
Chambersburg PA
CBHW020445220526
45464CB00002B/868